PICTURE LIBRARY

SHARKS

PICTURE LIBRARY
SHARKS

Norman B

Franklin Watts

London   New York   Sydney   Toronto

© 1989 Franklin Watts

First published in Great Britain
  1989 by
Franklin Watts
12a Golden Square
London W1R 4BA

First published in the USA by
Franklin Watts Inc
387 Park Avenue South
New York
NY 10016

First published in Australia by
Franklin Watts
14 Mars Road
Lane Cove
NSW 2066

UK ISBN: 0 86313 815 2
US ISBN: 0–531–10704–3
Library of Congress Catalog Card
Number 88–51516

Printed in Italy

Designed by
Barrett & Weintroub

Photographs by
Pat Morris
Planet Earth Pictures
Jack Jackson
Survival Anglia

Illustration by
Rhoda & Robert Burns

Technical Consultant
Michael Chinery

Contents

Introduction

Sharks are the great hunters of the world's seas and oceans. They are types of fish, and they prey on other fish and even other sharks.

There are more than 300 kinds of sharks. Many people are terrified of sharks, but only a few kinds of sharks are dangerous to humans.

Sharks live in all the world's oceans, but are most common in warm waters. They are fast swimmers and have a powerful bite.

△ A large shark glides smoothly through the water, fearing nothing. The only natural enemies of sharks are bigger sharks and man.

Sharks vary in size, shape and habits. The harmless whale shark may measure as much as 18 m (60 ft). Some kinds of dogfish shark are only a few inches long. Most sharks have a sleek, streamlined shape, ideal for speeding through the water.

Some sharks live in the depths of the ocean, while others are found in shallow waters. Many kinds of sharks lurk on the sea bed, feeding on shellfish.

△ A spotted dogfish, one of the smaller kinds of sharks. In many countries, dogfish are used for food.

Looking at sharks

Sharks differ from most other fish because they have no bones. Their skeleton is made of a tough, springy substance called cartilage. They do not have a gill cover like other fish, but have gill slits. The mouth of most kinds of shark is on the underside of the head. Most sharks have several rows of teeth.

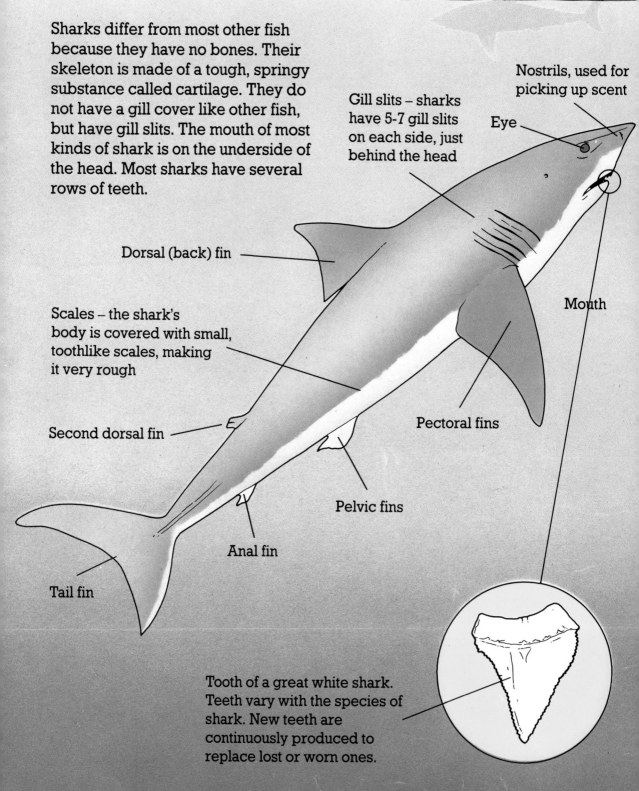

Nostrils, used for picking up scent

Gill slits – sharks have 5-7 gill slits on each side, just behind the head

Eye

Dorsal (back) fin

Mouth

Scales – the shark's body is covered with small, toothlike scales, making it very rough

Second dorsal fin

Pectoral fins

Pelvic fins

Anal fin

Tail fin

Tooth of a great white shark. Teeth vary with the species of shark. New teeth are continuously produced to replace lost or worn ones.

Heads

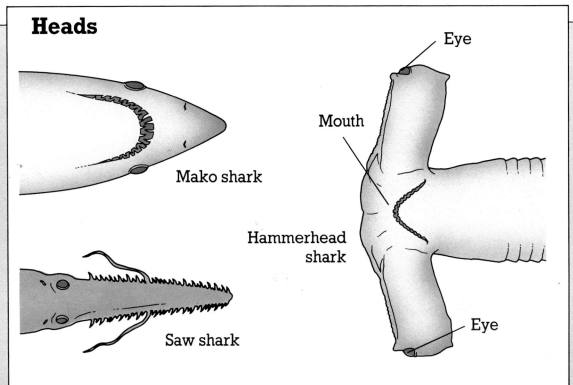

Mako shark

Saw shark

Eye

Mouth

Hammerhead
shark

Eye

Tails

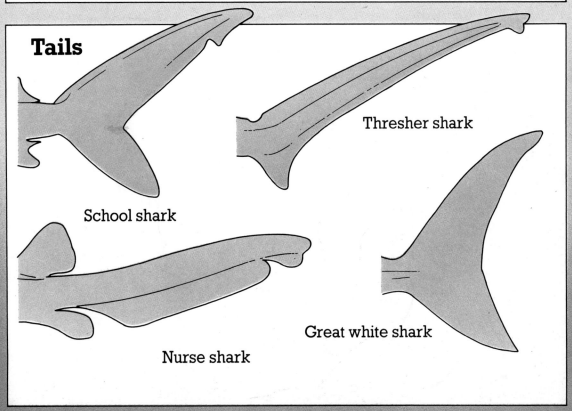

Thresher shark

School shark

Great white shark

Nurse shark

9

Birth of sharks

Baby sharks, called pups, begin life as eggs. In most species (kinds) of sharks, the eggs are hatched inside the mother's body.

Sharks have fewer young than most other fish. Some species have 50 or more pups, but most give birth to only a few at a time.

Only a few species of sharks, such as the hornshark and some dogfish, lay their eggs. Each egg is protected by a tough case.

▽ Two hornshark eggs lie well protected from the sea life crawling over them. It may be a few months before the baby sharks hatch and break out of the leathery cases enclosing them.

▷ A dogfish egg case (above), sometimes called a "mermaid's purse." Inside the hard case (below) can be seen the baby shark attached to a yolk. The threads attached to the case tangle in seaweed and stop it from being washed away.

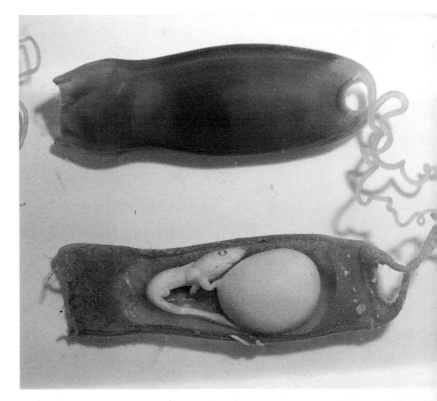

▽ A baby dogfish. The young of sharks look after themselves as soon as they are born.

Life of sharks

Sharks breathe oxygen from the water through organs called gills. They take in mouthfuls of water, which they pump over their gills by raising the floor of their mouth after closing it. The water passes out through the gill slits.

Most sharks must also keep swimming to stop themselves from sinking.

△ Many species of shark, such as this sand tiger shark, have backward-pointing teeth that dig deeply into their prey and prevent it escaping. The gill slits can be seen on the right.

Sharks have several rows of teeth in both jaws. They never stop growing their teeth. As teeth wear out or are lost, they are replaced by new teeth.

Teeth vary with different kinds of sharks. Some sharks have sharp cutting teeth, like razors, or pointed teeth to spear through small fish. Other sharks have flatter, grinding teeth for crushing the hard coverings of shellfish.

▽ The teeth of a whitepointer shark. They are pointed, with serrated (sawlike) edges, similar to those of its close relative, the great white shark. Experts can identify a species of shark by its teeth. Often this is the best way to tell similar species apart.

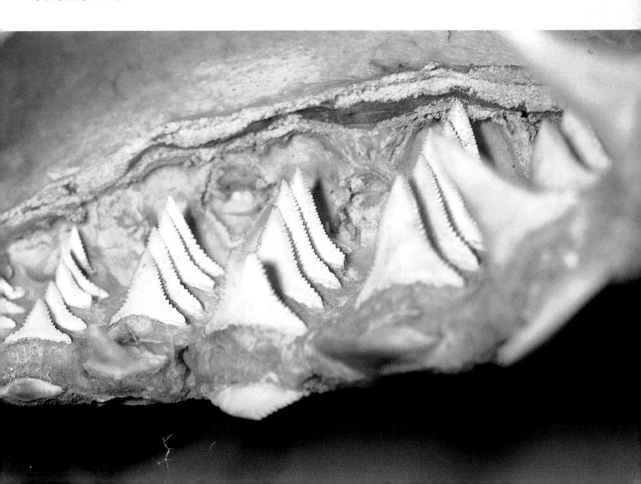

Sharks spend much of their time looking for food. Most sharks eat fish. They eat their prey whole or tear off large chunks of it. Many kinds of sharks eat squid and shellfish such as lobster and clams. Tiger sharks eat almost anything.

Large sharks eat sea animals such as seals, dolphins and other sharks. But the largest species, the basking and whale sharks, live only on tiny animal and plant life.

△ A basking shark swims through the water with its mouth open. Like many whales, these large animals live on tiny plant and animal life called plankton. They take in large gulps of water, and the plankton is strained out by their gills.

14

Most sharks are deadly hunters.
They have an excellent sense of
smell, and can detect the slightest
trace of blood from far away.

They move their head from side to
side as they pick up the scent of their
prey until they are close enough to
see it.

▽ A shark opens its
huge jaws to take in a
large fish.

Some species of sharks hunt in packs. But the larger sharks usually hunt alone. When two or more sharks go for the same prey, a fight may start. The smell of blood attracts more sharks, and a wounded shark may be eaten by others.

Sharks are often accompanied by smaller fish. The remora, or shark sucker, can cling to a shark by means of a suction pad on top of its head.

△ Several remoras swim along with a bullshark. The suction pad on the lowest fish can be seen clearly. Remoras feed on small creatures attached to the shark's skin and sometimes eat scraps from the shark's own meal. Known as "ocean hitchhikers," they must be quick and elusive to avoid being eaten themselves.

▷ A gray reef shark with a remora attached under its belly.

The larger sharks are so fierce that they have few natural enemies. They are rarely approached by other predators.

Smaller sharks, especially the bottom dwellers, have markings that help them to blend in with their surroundings. Leopard sharks and nurse sharks, for example, can stay on the seabed, hidden from enemies and their own prey. The swell shark can puff up its body to look bigger and fiercer than it is.

▽ The swell shark is a small bottom-dwelling shark of the Pacific, about 60–90 cm (2–3 ft) long. It can fill its stomach with air or water to give itself a more frightening appearance.

Sharks usually approach their prey with caution, especially anything large or unusual. Unless they are really hungry, they will circle round it for some time before attacking.

Experienced divers have learned to swim with sharks and feed them, even some of the dangerous ones. They can usually tell whether a shark is in an aggressive mood by the way it moves in toward them.

△ A shark approaches a diver from behind. Divers must have their wits about them when sharks are around. When the water is not very clear, they can appear seemingly out of nowhere, from any direction.

"Maneaters"

Many people regard sharks as maneaters. Perhaps only the great white shark deserves this reputation. It can measure about 6 m (20 ft) long and feeds on large prey such as sea lions and other sharks. White sharks will attack human beings and even small boats.

Other kinds of sharks have been known to attack humans and even the smallest sharks may bite if disturbed.

▷ A great white shark rises out of the water to collect bait dangled from a line. The only safe way to study these awesome creatures is from a sturdy boat or underwater, from inside a strong cage.

▽ The tiger shark is feared because it will attack anything in the water, including humans. It is sometimes called the "garbage can of the sea" because of its habit of feeding off any trash thrown from ships.

All kinds of sharks

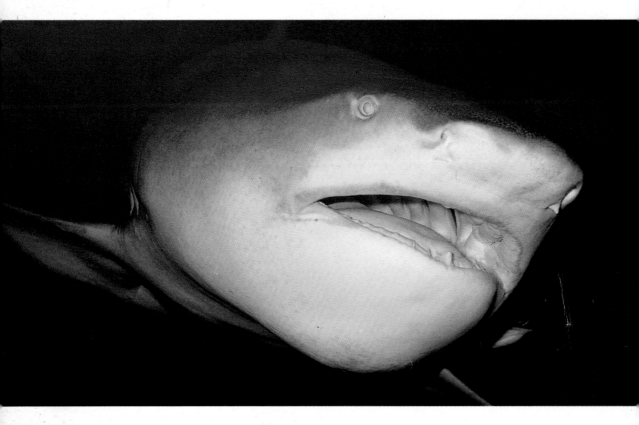

Scientists have named more than 300 species of sharks. New species are often identified.

Sometimes, sharks that had been thought of as different species are found to be the same. The coloring of a species of shark might vary in different parts of the world's oceans. Coloration might also change when a young shark becomes an adult, as when the tiger shark loses its stripes.

△ A lemon shark from the warm waters of the Atlantic. It grows to more than 3 m (10 ft) and can be very dangerous if provoked.

▷ A hammerhead shark (above) and a closeup (below) of the smooth hammerhead. The several species of hammerhead are among the most curious looking sharks, with eye and nostril set on lobes at each end of its head.

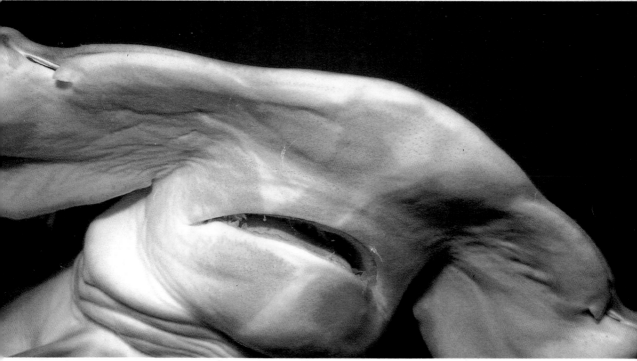

△ Blacktip reef sharks have black tips on all fins. They are small sharks, usually under 1.5 m (5 ft), and are not normally dangerous. They are found in the Red Sea and the warm waters of the Indian and Pacific oceans.

◁ The nurse shark is a large bottom-dweller, measuring as much as 4.3 m (14 ft). It has a barbel, a kind of feeler for locating prey, on each side of its snout.

▷ The gray reef shark lives in the Red Sea and the Indian and Pacific oceans. Although less than about 1.5 m (5 ft) long, gray reef sharks are considered dangerous, especially those found in the Pacific.

▽ The sand tiger shark is found in shallow waters in the Atlantic and the Mediterranean. It grows to about 3 m (10 ft) but is not particularly dangerous.

There are more than 30 species of dogfish, the smallest members of the shark family. Few grow to more than about 1 m (3 ft). They range from the kinds common in shallow coastal waters to deepwater species that are rarely seen.

Most kinds of dogfish are harmless to humans. They feed on almost anything smaller than themselves, such as worms, small fish and shellfish.

▽ The leopard shark is among the largest dogfish, growing to as much as 1.5 m (5 ft). It gets its name from its spotty markings, and is able to rest on the sea bed where it blends in with its surroundings. It is particularly common off the American Pacific coast.

△ The smooth-hound is one of several species of dogfish without spines. Another group of dogfish, with spines in front of their dorsal fins, are called spiny dogfish.

▷ Viewed from beneath, the large-spotted dogfish looks much like a shark. It usually grows to no more than 1 m (3 ft), although larger specimens, up to 1.5 m (5 ft), have been found.

The story of sharks

△ Hunting the harmless basking shark in Scotland over a hundred years ago.

Shark ancestors

The first true sharks swam the seas about 350 million years ago. These were the ancestors of the sharks we know today. They have changed very little since that time, even surviving the age of dinosaurs, when large, fierce reptiles made their home in the seas.

Some species of sharks became extinct (died out). Fossil teeth, 14 cm (5.5 in) long and similar to those of the great white shark, have been found of a shark that swam the seas less than a million years ago. This fearsome giant, called megalodon, must have been 13 m (43 ft) long, twice the size of the largest known great white sharks.

Relatives

A major difference between sharks and other fish is that the skeleton of sharks is made of cartilage, not bone. Other fish are sometimes referred to as bony fish, the sharks as cartilaginous fish. The closest relatives of sharks include skates and rays, which also belong to the cartilaginous group.

The shark industry

Shark fishing began in many places around the world as a

△ A cargo of sharks thrown away by a Japanese fishing boat. Sometimes sharks are caught in fishing nets when they are not wanted.

minor industry. The flesh of some sharks is eaten and the skin makes a durable leather. The industry grew in the late 1920s when it was discovered that sharks' liver is a source of vitamin A. When scientists discovered a chemical method for making vitamin A, the shark industry declined again.

But stocks of other fish in the earth's oceans have become short because of overfishing. So fishing fleets are again turning to sharks.

Fear of sharks

Stories of ferocious shark attacks told by sailors and fishermen over the years have made the shark into the savage monster portrayed in movies. Since people fear sharks, there is very little protest when sharks are killed.

Protection

But most kinds of sharks are not harmful to human beings. Many that are thought to be so are dangerous only when disturbed. Fishermen might tell of the tremendous fight sharks put up when hooked or speared, and how terrifying their bite is. But this is understandable, because

△ A diver has come out of his observation cage to feed a blue shark. Experts have found that many species regarded for years as dangerous are harmless if approached with caution and treated with care.

they are fighting for their lives. Those same fishermen find it hard to believe that divers can mix with so-called dangerous sharks underwater without being attacked, and even feed them by hand.

Sharks do not reproduce as quickly as other fish. Nearly 100 million sharks are killed every year, and many species are in danger of extinction. Sharks have the right to be protected from wholesale and wasteful slaughter as much as any other animal.

Facts and records

△ The first bigmouth shark discovered is displayed in a showcase in a Los Angeles museum.

New species

We do not know exactly how many species of sharks there are. New species are always being identified. As recently as 1976, a specimen of a large, unidentified shark was found entangled in the anchor cables of a United States Navy research ship off Hawaii. It was 4.5 m (15 ft) long, with lots of tiny teeth in a huge mouth. It was nicknamed "bigmouth" or "megamouth."

Bigmouth was found to live on deepsea shrimp, filtering food from great gulps of water like those other huge sharks, the basking and whale sharks. But it is very different from any other shark, and scientists have placed it in a family of its own. A second bigmouth shark was caught off California in 1984.

Tough teeth

The teeth of the great white and some other sharks are made of the hardest substance that comes from any animal. They are about as tough as stainless steel.

When a shark like the great white bites, the triangular teeth in its upper jaw mesh perfectly with those in the lower jaw. The bite has a force of 3,000 kg per sq cm (½ ton per sq inch).

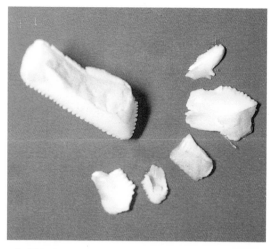

△ Fragments of shark teeth taken from the flesh of victims.

Glossary

Bait
Anything used by photographers, scientists or fishermen to attract sharks or other fish, usually in the form of food.

Barbel
A kind of feeler. Some bottom-dwelling sharks have a barbel on each side of their snout to help them find prey on the sea bottom.

Bony fish
A general term commonly used to distinguish most of the other fish from the sharks. Most fish have a bony skeleton, whereas the skeletons of sharks consist of cartilage.

Cartilage
A hard, rubbery substance, sometimes known as gristle. It makes up the skeleton of sharks. Human beings have cartilage at the tip of the nose, for example, and in some joints.

Extinct
An extinct species is one that has died out.

Fins
Sharks and other aquatic animals swim, balance and steer their bodies by means of fins.

Fossil
Any remains or impressions of ancient living things preserved in rock.

Gills
Organs in sharks and other fish that filter the oxygen out of water and enable them to breathe.

Gill slits
The openings for the expulsion of water after it has passed through the gills.

Pup
A baby shark.

Remoras
Small fish that swim along with sharks and other large sea creatures, often attaching themselves to the underside of the shark by means of a sucker on the top of their head.

Species
A particular kind of animal. Animals of the same species breed young of that species.

Zooplankton
The mass of tiny animal and plant life that lives in the oceans, mainly on or near the surface.

Index